Squares and Triangles

Kay Robertson

Rourke
Educational Media

rourkeeducationalmedia.com

*Scan for Related Titles
and Teacher Resources*

Teaching Focus:

Concept Words- Locate all the shape words used in the book. What shape words are missing?

Before Reading:

Building Academic Vocabulary and Background Knowledge

Before reading a book, it is important to set the stage for your child or student by using pre-reading strategies. This will help them develop their vocabulary, increase their reading comprehension, and make connections across the curriculum.

1. Read the title and look at the cover. *Let's make predictions about what this book will be about.*
2. Take a picture walk by talking about the pictures/photographs in the book. Implant the vocabulary as you take the picture walk. Be sure to talk about the text features such as headings, Table of Contents, glossary, bolded words, captions, charts/diagrams, or Index.
3. Have students read the first page of text with you then have students read the remaining text.
4. Strategy Talk – use to assist students while reading.
   - Get your mouth ready
   - Look at the picture
   - Think…does it make sense
   - Think…does it look right
   - Think…does it sound right
   - Chunk it – by looking for a part you know
5. Read it again.
6. After reading the book complete the activities below.

High Frequency Words

Flip through the book and locate how many times the high frequency words were used.

can
make
squares
triangles
you

After Reading:

Comprehension and Extension Activity

After reading the book, work on the following questions with your child or students in order to check their level of reading comprehension and content mastery.

1. *How can squares turn into a rectangle?* (Inferring)
2. *Explain the difference between a square and a triangle.* (Summarize)
3. *What objects at home or school are made of squares and triangles?* (Text to self connection)
4. *What shapes can you make with triangles?* (Visualizing)

Extension Activity

Go on a shape hunt! Walk around your classroom or home and search for objects made with squares and triangles. Draw a picture of the objects in your notebook. How many objects did you find?

Triangles and squares are everywhere! Triangles have three sides, but squares have more. They have four equal sides.

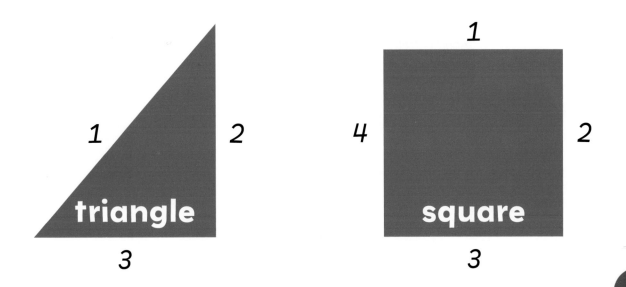

1 2
triangle
3

1
4 2
square
3

Let's see what we can make using squares and triangles.

What can you make with two triangles?

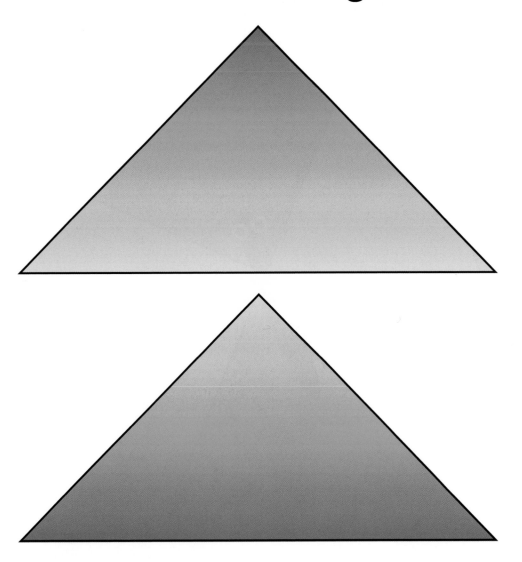

A butterfly!

What can you make with six squares?

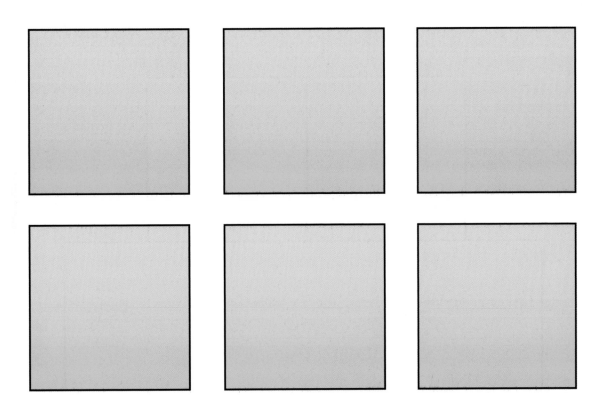

A pyramid!

What can you make with two squares and one triangle?

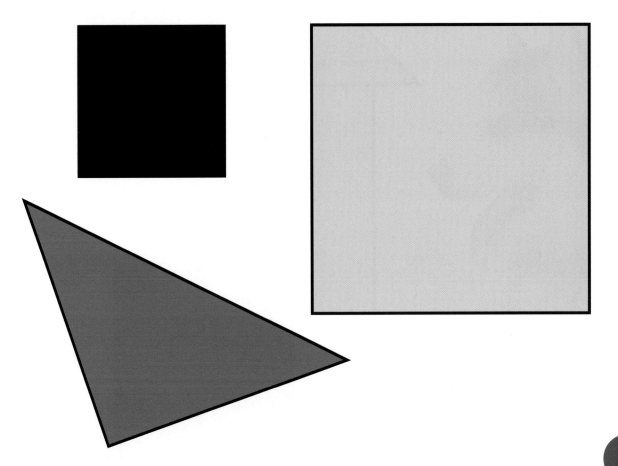

A dog house!

What can you make with one square and two triangles?

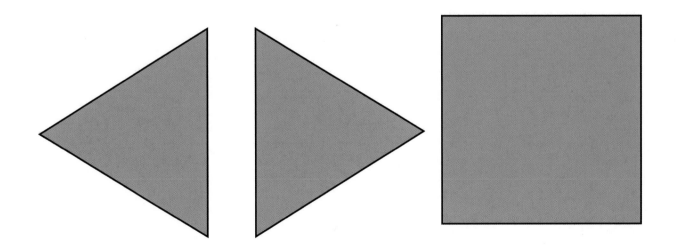

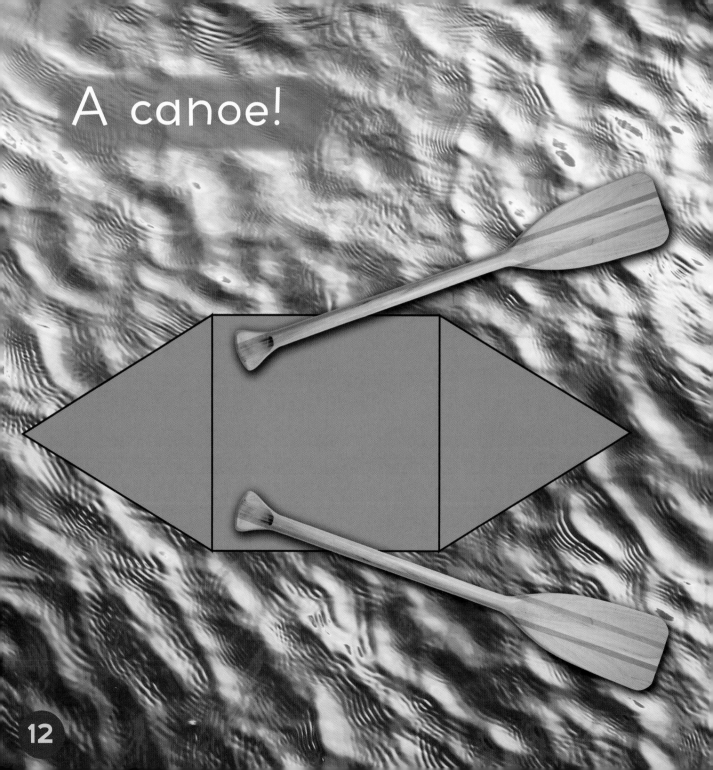

A canoe!

What can you make with two squares and three triangles?

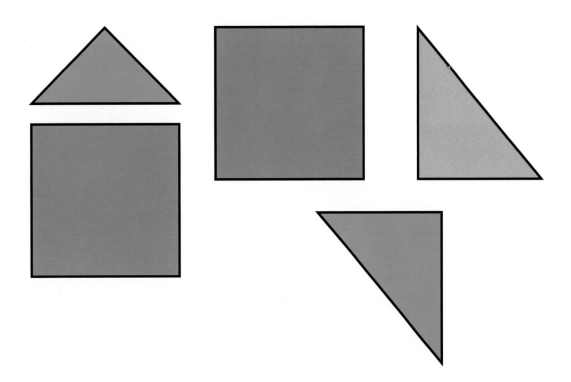

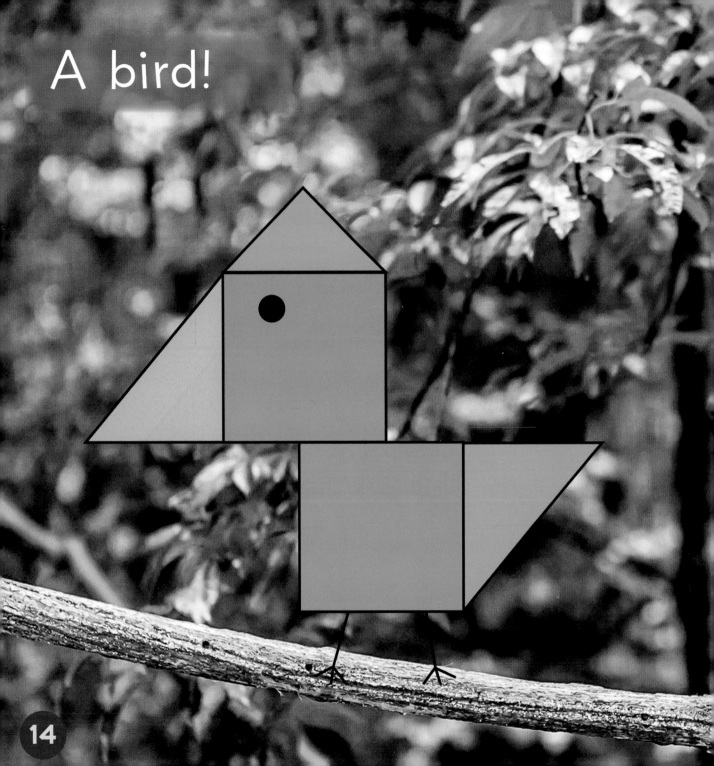

A bird!

What can you make with eight triangles?

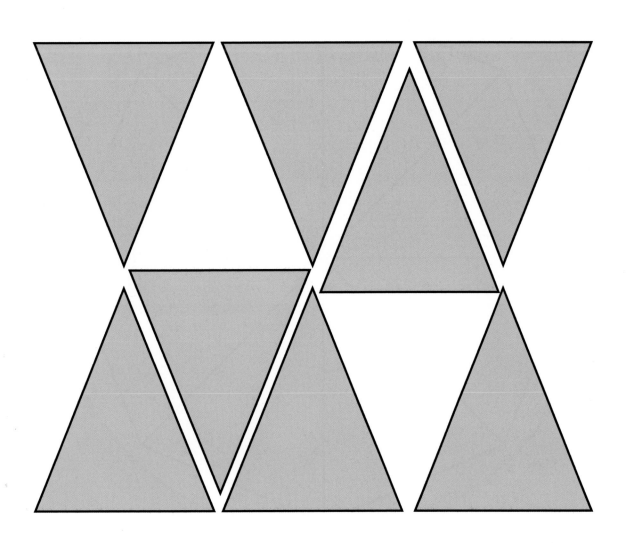

A pizza!

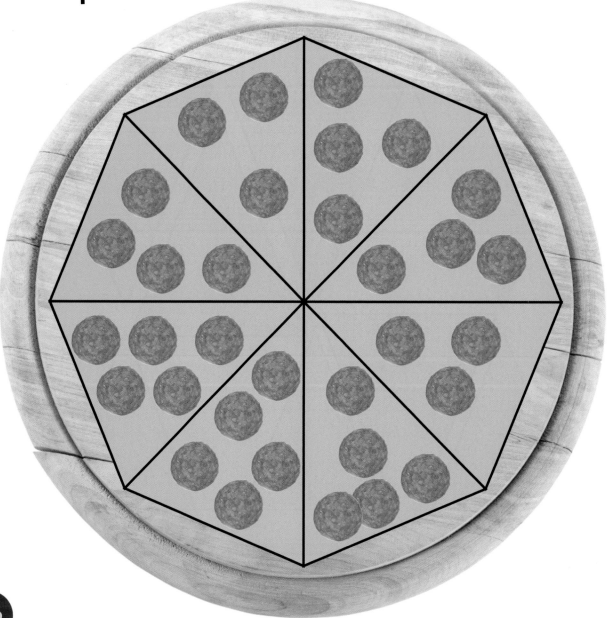

What can you make
with four squares and
five triangles?

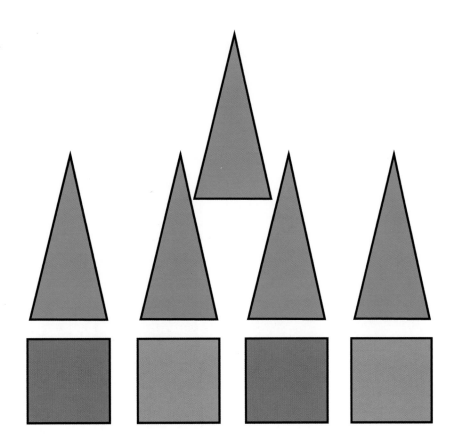

A palm tree!

What can you make
with three squares
and three triangles?

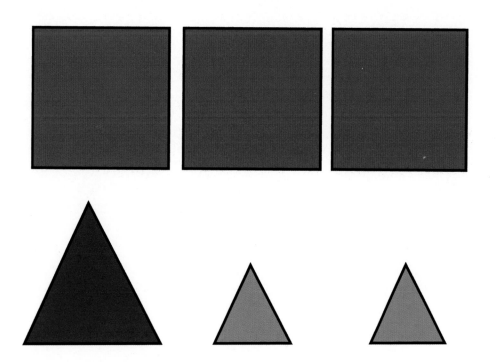

A rocket!

What can you make with four squares and six triangles?

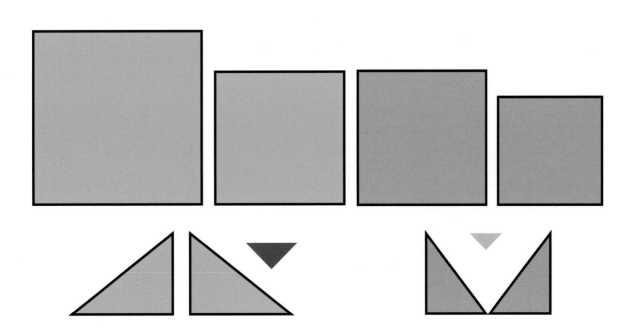

A dog and a cat!

Now it is your turn to see what you can make with squares and triangles.

Index

Websites

http://pbskids.org/games/shapes/
http://www.abcya.com/shape_match.htm
http://www.ixl.com/math/kindergarten/
  identify-shapes

Meet The Author!
www.meetREMauthors.com

About the Author

Kay Robertson lives in Florida with her family. On Friday nights, they eat triangle pizza slices and watch a movie and on Sunday mornings she makes square waffles for breakfast. Yum!

www.rourkeeducationalmedia.com

PHOTO CREDITS: Cover and page 22 photo © maxstockphoto, cover animal faces © Igor Zakowski; illustrations with shapes by Christian Lopetz; photos: page 6 © Smileus; page 8 © Waj; page 10 © xmee; page 12 © Kazakov Maksim and Mega Pixel; page 14 © MarcusVDT; page 16 © aboikis, Lucie Lang; page 18 © Pakhnyushchy; page 20 © puchan; page 23 © Patrick Foto; Edited by: Luana Mitten

Cover design and Interior design: by Nicola Stratford
www.nicolastratford.com

Library of Congress PCN Data

Squares and Triangles / Kay Robertson
(Concepts)
ISBN 978-1-63430-052-0 (hard cover)
ISBN 978-1-63430-082-7 (soft cover)
ISBN 978-1-63430-110-7 (e-Book)
Library of Congress Control Number: 2014953317

Rourke Educational Media
Printed in the United States of America, North Mankato, Minnesota

Also Available as: